BOTANICAL
Beauty

AUBRE ANDRUS

80
ESSENTIAL RECIPES
for Natural Spa Products

CONTENTS

INTRODUCTION

Creating a spa experience at home is easier than
you think. Believe it or not, you'll find a lot of what
you need in the kitchen! The recipes in this book
aren't much different from traditional recipes
(such as those for cupcakes, cookies and cake), but
these recipes aren't meant to be eaten. Instead of
soothing your sweet tooth, these recipes soothe
your body, from your head to your toes!

From sensitive skin to dry hair to chapped lips, there are plenty of products in this book that can exfoliate and moisturize. If you have sore muscles, there's a natural recipe that can help relieve the aching. And if you're just looking for some sweet-smelling spa products that will help you relax or re-energize, a pillow mist or hair perfume spray might be perfect for you.

Flip through these pages to find your favourite recipes in the same way you'd flip through a cookbook. There's no wrong or right place to start. There's a homemade beauty product for everyone, from lotion and balms to sprays and soaks to headbands and hair ties. We even added some essential oils to these recipes so your DIY spa experience is as relaxing as the real thing.

At the end of the book, you'll find ways to label and package your products, and some tips for perfecting at-home pedicures and manicures.

IT'S TIME TO PAMPER YOURSELF!

SPECIALITY INGREDIENTS

Many of the recipes in this book call for simple ingredients that you probably already have, such as bicarbonate of soda, olive oil or vanilla extract. But there are some speciality ingredients that you probably won't find at home.

Luckily, they can be found at health food shops or some supermarkets near the spices, pharmacy or beauty aisles. (Or shop online!) Here are some of those ingredients and the reasons you need them in your recipes.

beeswax pastilles

aloe vera gel

Epsom salts

Aloe vera gel — *Aloe vera gel moisturizes skin and hair, and it can help to soothe sunburns with a natural cooling effect.*

Beeswax — *Beeswax helps to firm balms and creams. These recipes call for grated beeswax, which can be made by using a cheese grater on a bar of pure beeswax. Or you could buy beeswax pastilles, which are small granules or pellets.*

Citric acid — *Citric acid is a powder that helps to create a fizz in bath and shower products. It can be found in some supermarkets and high street shops.*

Coconut oil — *Coconut oil moisturizes your skin and hair.*

Distilled water — *Distilled water has been boiled to remove impurities, and it will help your ingredients last longer. It can be bought online. Always use distilled water in these recipes rather than tap water.*

Epsom salts — *Epsom salts soothe aching muscles and relieve itching.*

Jojoba oil — *Jojoba oil is soothing when applied to irritated skin, from acne to sunburn.*

Rosewater — *Rosewater soothes and strengthens skin, and it also conditions hair. It has a floral aroma.*

Sea salt — *The rough texture of sea salt helps to exfoliate skin while naturally detoxifying.*

Shea butter — *Shea butter moisturizes, soothes and balances skin without clogging pores. It can even help to heal cuts and scrapes.*

Vegetable glycerine — *Vegetable glycerine naturally attracts moisture when applied to skin.*

Witch hazel — *Witch hazel soothes itchy or irritated skin, including acne and some foot rashes and infections. It can also tighten and moisturize skin.*

ESSENTIAL OILS

Many of the recipes in this book call for essential oils. Essential oils are used for aromatherapy (they smell lovely and can make you feel great) and for health benefits for your hair, skin and body.

They can be found at health food shops, some high street shops or online. Here are the essential oils used in this book and the reasons you might use them in your recipes.

Lavender
Lavender is probably the most popular essential oil. It can soothe skin and possibly help to fight acne. It has a floral aroma that can help you to fall asleep.

Roman Chamomile
Roman chamomile essential oil soothes skin and has a calming aroma that can help you to wind down and clear your sinuses.

Lemon*
Lemon essential oil is antibacterial. It can prevent infection when applied to the skin. Its citrus aroma is energizing.

Orange*

Orange essential oil is a natural cleanser and deodorizer, and it can help to heal skin. Like lemon, its citrus aroma is energizing.

Peppermint

Peppermint essential oil has a cooling effect. It can relieve muscle pain and has an invigorating aroma that can make you feel alert.

Tea Tree

Tea tree oil fights bacteria, fungi and viruses, so it can help to treat athlete's foot, acne and more when applied to the skin.

Be careful! Don't allow any undiluted essential oil to get on your skin or in your eyes or mouth. Recipes from this book containing essential oils should not be used on children under the age of 6, and for older children, an adult's help is recommended.

*Lemon and orange essential oils could be phototoxic, which means they can make your skin extra-sensitive to the sun. Don't apply citrus essential oils to bare skin before going outside. And always wear sunscreen!

MEASURING YOUR INGREDIENTS

Essential oils are very potent and must be diluted with distilled water or a carrier oil, such as coconut oil, jojoba oil or olive oil. It might not seem like you're using a lot, but a little goes a long way!

The recipes in this book dilute the essential oil to about 1 per cent. That means some recipes require only a few drops. We measure essential oils by the drop in this book because it's hard to measure any other way. (There are 20 drops in 1 millilitre, and ¼ teaspoon is a little more than 1 millilitre.) There are very few recipes that will require more than ¼ teaspoon of essential oil.

coconut oil

jojoba oil

olive oil

HOW TO SAFELY MELT BUTTER AND OIL

Shea butter is a soft solid that must be melted for many recipes in this book. A double boiler is best for melting oils and butters, but you can also microwave them at 50 per cent power in 30-second increments – and stir in between – until the solid is almost all the way melted. Stir to complete the melting process. You don't want to overheat the oils or butters.

Coconut oil is also used often in this book. Whether your coconut oil is a solid or a liquid depends on where you live, what time of year it is and the air temperature. To solidify it, place it in the refrigerator until it hardens. To liquefy it, heat it in a microwave-safe bowl in 10-second increments at 50 per cent power – and stir in between – until the solid is almost all the way melted.

It's best to heat the solids in a microwave-safe bowl with a pourable spout and a handle, like a glass Pyrex measuring jug. Make sure you always wear oven gloves when removing a hot bowl from the microwave.

HOW TO SAFELY STORE YOUR PRODUCTS

It's best to use glass containers, not plastic, to store any recipe that contains essential oils, because the essential oils can deteriorate plastic over time. All of the recipes in this book make small batches as they are natural and don't contain preservatives.

Unless indicated otherwise, the finished products should be stored in a cool, dry place and should be used within 2 to 4 weeks. Never use a recipe if it looks like it has grown mould, if it has changed colours or if it begins to smell bad.

ALLERGIES

Some people have skin sensitivities and allergies. Check with your doctor or dermatologist before using any of these recipes.

CLEAN UP

Many of the recipes in this book use oils and butters, which might feel greasy. To clean up, wipe your hands and any used dishes with dry kitchen roll first, then use soap and water to wash. When using recipes in the bath, such as sugar scrubs, wipe the floor clean with a dry towel afterwards. Oils and butters can make surfaces slippery and unsafe.

WHERE TO FIND PACKAGING FOR YOUR PRODUCTS

It's important to use brand new containers to store your products. It will help prevent mould from growing. Here's where you can buy containers that are perfect for the recipes in this book:

• reusable 60-ml glass bottles or 120-ml glass containers can be found in the essential oil aisle at health food shops

• reusable 60-ml plastic spray bottles or 90-ml plastic squeeze bottles can be found in the travel section of chemists or supermarkets

• reusable 120-ml spice tins or empty spice jars can be found in the bulk spice aisle in supermarkets or health food shops

• 250-ml glass jars can be found in the jam or canning aisle in supermarkets or health food shops

• round plastic containers with screw-top lids can be found in the jewellery or bead storage aisle at craft shops or in the travel aisle of department stores

Hands and *feet*

This section is full of recipes that will pamper your hands and feet. From dry, itchy skin to tired toes, there are plenty of recipes for soothing creams, scrubs and soaks that will help you to heal. After all, looking beautiful is all about feeling beautiful!

cuticle balm

foot soak

sore muscle butter

Chocolate Sugar Hand Scrub

You will need:

115 g white sugar
100 g brown sugar
1 tsp baking cocoa
3 tbsp olive oil
½ tsp vanilla extract

This scrub smells good enough to eat – and technically, you could! It turns out that sugar is great for polishing your hands. To use, spoon a scoop into your hands and rub hands together gently over a sink. Rinse, then pat hands dry with a clean towel.

DIRECTIONS:

Mix all ingredients in a bowl. Scoop into a lidded glass container. Store in a cool, dry place. Use within 3–4 weeks.

Cuticle Balms

No more dry cuticles! Give your nails extra attention and help prevent hangnails with these soothing balms. One recipe makes enough to fill several small containers, so you can give these away as gifts too! To use, massage on and around your nails three times per week.

Strengthening Lavender Balm

Moisturize and soften your cuticles, or the skin around your nails, and strengthen the nail itself with this lovely smelling balm.

beeswax pastilles

You will need:

6 tsp shea butter
3 tsp grated beeswax or
    beeswax pastilles
3 tsp jojoba oil
3 drops lavender essential oil

Whitening Lemon Balm

This cuticle balm goes a step further and can help whiten stained or yellowing nails, thanks to the lemon essential oil.

You will need:

6 tsp shea butter
3 tsp grated beeswax or
    beeswax pastilles
3 tsp jojoba oil
3 drops lemon essential oil

DIRECTIONS:

Scoop shea butter and beeswax into a microwave-safe bowl with a pourable spout. Microwave in 30-second increments at 50 per cent power, stirring each time, until mixture mostly liquefies. Remove bowl with oven gloves and stir until clear, not cloudy. Add jojoba oil and stir. Let cool slightly, then add essential oil.

Carefully pour into small lidded containers. Let harden at room temperature. Makes enough to fill about six small circular containers. Store in a cool, dry place. Use within 3–4 weeks.

Hand Creams

Here's a moisturizing balm that will turn dry hands soft and shimmering – and it smells good too. To use, scoop a small amount into your palm. Massage hands together, working the lotion from your fingertips to your wrists. If your hands feel too oily, wipe them with a tissue.

Cooling Peppermint Hand Cream

This balm softens your skin and leaves it feeling cool – and don't forget about that invigorating minty scent!

jojoba oil

You will need:

55 g shea butter
1 tbsp beeswax or beeswax
   pastilles
30 ml jojoba oil
6 drops peppermint essential oil

Lavender Cream for Dry Hands

Lavender has a moisturizing effect on even the driest skin, but that's not all. Its floral scent is known to be curiously calming.

You will need:

55 g shea butter
1 tbsp beeswax or beeswax
   pastilles
30 ml jojoba oil
6 drops lavender essential oil

DIRECTIONS:

Scoop shea butter and beeswax into a microwave-safe bowl with a pourable spout. Microwave in 30-second increments at 50 per cent power, stirring each time, until mixture mostly liquefies. Remove bowl with oven gloves and stir until clear, not cloudy. Add jojoba oil and stir. Let cool slightly, then add essential oil.

Carefully pour mixture into lidded glass jar. Let solidify at room temperature overnight. Store in a cool, dry place. Use within 3–4 weeks.

Nail-Strengthening Serum

You will need:

4 tbsp jojoba oil
2 tbsp olive oil
10 drops lavender essential oil
5 drops lemon essential oil

There's nothing better for dry nails than jojoba oil. To use, add one drop to each nail, then massage onto the nail, under the nail and around the cuticle. Apply this serum three days in a row or until your nails feel moisturized and strong.

olive oil

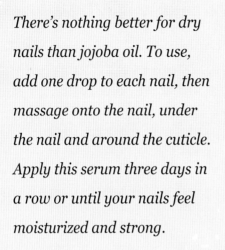

DIRECTIONS:

Mix all ingredients together in a bowl with a pourable spout. Pour into a glass bottle that has a dropper. Makes enough to fill a 90-ml bottle. Store in a cool, dry place. Use within 3–4 weeks.

Warming Wrap

You will need:

- 40 g oats
- ¼ tsp cinnamon
- ¼ tsp cayenne pepper
- 1 tbsp honey
- 1 tbsp olive oil
- 1–2 tbsp warm distilled water
- 3 drops orange essential oil (optional)
- 2 flannels

Slather this naturally warming paste onto your feet or your hands. Finish by wrapping each hand or foot with a warm flannel. (Run warm water over a flannel, then wring out the excess water.) Ask a friend to help with the last step. Leave on for 10 minutes, then rinse hands or feet in a bowl of water and pat dry with a clean towel.

DIRECTIONS:

Mix oats in a blender. Pour into a bowl, then stir in cinnamon, cayenne pepper, honey, olive oil and essential oil. Stir in water until mixture reaches desired consistency. Makes enough paste for a mask for your hands or feet.

Sea Salt Hand Scrubs

This scrub is perfect for chapped winter hands. The coarse sea salt helps to scrub off dead skin cells, and the olive oil will leave your skin feeling silky smooth. To use, spoon a small amount into palms. Rub hands together over the sink, working the mixture into your skin. Rinse, then pat hands dry with a clean towel.

Energizing Citrus Scrub

This citrus scrub smells bright, sweet and squeaky clean!

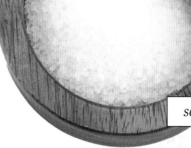

You will need:

270 g sea salt
120 ml olive oil
15–20 drops lemon or
orange essential oil

sea salt

Antibacterial Hand Scrub

The tea tree essential oil in this recipe can help to kill bacteria and fungus as well as alleviate itchiness.

You will need:

270 g sea salt
120 ml olive oil
15–20 drops tea tree essential oil

DIRECTIONS:

Mix all ingredients in a bowl. Scoop into a lidded glass container. Stir before each use. Store in a cool, dry place. Use within 3–4 weeks.

DIY
Nail Art

You will need:

plastic sandwich bag
small manicure scissors
coloured nail polish
clear nail polish
toothpick (optional)

It's so hard to paint your own nails perfectly, isn't it? Not anymore! Create your own press-on looks that look, well, perfect! Make tiny nail stickers that can easily jazz up a simple polish job. You'll paint tiny details onto a sandwich bag instead of your hand, which makes it a whole lot easier.

DIRECTIONS:

Paint a rectangle of clear nail polish onto a plastic sandwich bag. This will be your "canvas". Let dry for 5 minutes. Now paint 10 small designs – one for each nail – using coloured polish on top of the dried clear polish. A toothpick is helpful for tiny details and can be used like a brush if you first place a small dot of nail polish on the sandwich bag. Once you have finished your designs, let dry overnight.

Carefully peel entire rectangle from bag. To use, cut out stickers with small manicure scissors. Paint a coat of clear or coloured polish onto your nail, then place the sticker on top. Let dry. Finish with a coat of clear polish. Let dry.

To make a heart:
Drop a small dot of nail polish onto the surface. Use a toothpick to push the nail polish to form a rounded edge to the top left and top right, and then to a point at the bottom centre.

To make a flower:
Drop a large dot of nail polish onto the surface. Use a toothpick to push the nail polish outwards to form five rounded edges. Let dry. Drop a small dot of nail polish in a different colour in the centre.

Press-On Nail Wraps

You will need:

plastic sandwich bag
coloured nail polish
clear nail polish
permanent marker
toothpick (optional)

These nail wraps are simple to make but can add a lot of flair to your nails! Experiment with colours and designs until you find a combination you love.

DIRECTIONS:

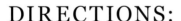

Open a sandwich bag and slide your hand inside. Using a permanent marker, outline the shape of each of your nails. Flip the bag over. Following the nail stencil, paint nail polish within the lines. Make sure it's a thick enough layer that you will be able to peel it off in the future. You might need multiple coats of polish.

Let the nail polish dry, then top it with a design. A toothpick is helpful when making small details, such as polka dots. Place a small dot of nail polish on the bag, then use your toothpick like a brush. Let dry overnight.

Carefully peel each wrap from bag. To use, paint your nails with a clear coat of nail polish first, then press on the decal while clear coat is still wet. If any excess decal hangs over the edge of your nail, trim with small manicure scissors or file away excess decal once the clear nail polish is dry.

Foot Soaks for Tired Toes

Give your feet a break! To use, fill a large bowl (big enough to fit both your feet) halfway with warm water. Pour half of the mix into the bowl. Let your feet soak for 10–15 minutes, then pat dry with a clean towel. Discard the remaining liquid in the sink.

Re-energizing Mix

Bring your feet back to life after a long day. The peppermint in this soak will put some pep in your step!

You will need:

220 g bicarbonate of soda
125 g Epsom salts
10 drops peppermint essential oil

bicarbonate of soda

Epsom salts

Soothing Soak

Sensitive skin? This soak will calm and repair, as well as relax your mind, thanks to the spa-like scent of lavender.

You will need:

106 g powdered milk
125 g Epsom salts
5 drops lavender essential oil
  (optional)
3 drops orange essential oil
  (optional)

DIRECTIONS:

Mix all ingredients in a bowl, then pour into a lidded glass container until ready to use. Each recipe makes enough for two foot soaks.

Gingerbread Foot Scrub

You will need:

115 g white sugar
100 g brown sugar
3 tbsp olive oil
½ tsp ginger
¼ tsp cinnamon
¼ tsp allspice
¼ tsp nutmeg
½ tsp vanilla extract

ginger

This mix won't make a batch of cookies, but it will make another sweet treat – for your feet! This scrub can also make a great gift when packaged in a pretty glass container.

To use, massage a scoop onto your feet while sitting over a bath or a large bowl of water. Rinse, then pat feet dry with a clean towel.

Be careful! Oils and butters can make bath surfaces slippery. A non-slip bath mat may help. Wipe bath with a dry towel when finished.

DIRECTIONS:

Mix all ingredients in a small bowl. Scoop into a lidded glass container. Store in a cool, dry place, and use within 3–4 weeks.

Cooling Sore Muscle Butter

You will need:

120 ml coconut oil
105 g shea butter
10 drops peppermint
  essential oil
15 drops tea tree essential oil

Pamper sore feet and tired toes. This butter melts as you massage it into your skin. Thanks to the peppermint and tea tree essential oils, it has a nice cooling effect. To use, massage a small scoop onto feet and lower legs.

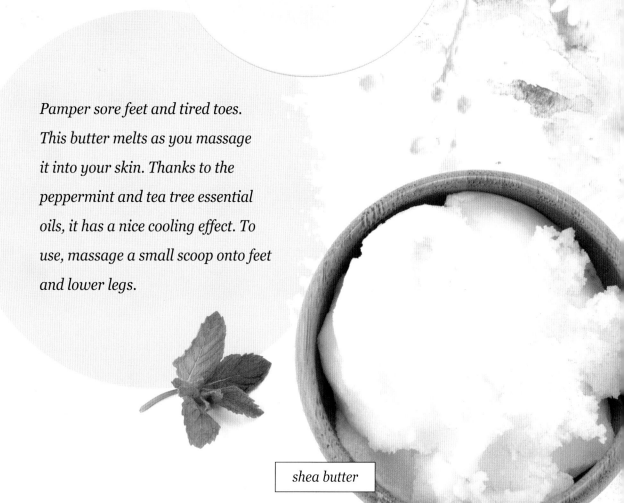

shea butter

DIRECTIONS:

Scoop coconut oil and shea butter into a microwave-safe mixing bowl. Microwave in 30-second increments at 50 per cent power, stirring each time, until mixture mostly liquefies. Remove bowl with oven gloves and stir until clear, not cloudy.

To turn the mixture into cream, cover bowl with cling film and let cool in refrigerator until the texture resembles softened butter (this step should take no longer than an hour). If mixture fully hardens, remove from refrigerator and let it warm on the worktop. Add essential oil, then whip with a hand mixer on low speed for 3–5 minutes, or until the colour brightens and peaks form in the mixture.

When desired consistency is reached, scoop into jar with spatula. Store in a cool, dry place. Use within 3–4 weeks.

Foot Repair Stick

You will need:

80 ml coconut oil

75 g grated beeswax or beeswax pastilles

3 tbsp shea butter

16 drops tea tree essential oil (optional)

empty deodorant tube

Give your feet a break! Roll this soothing balm onto your feet before bed, focusing on dry, cracked heels. Rub in the excess balm with your fingers, then slip into a warm pair of socks. When your feet hit the floor in the morning, they'll be soft and smooth!

coconut oil

beeswax pastilles

Be careful! Don't pour any remaining mixture down the drain — it could cause a clog. Instead, let it harden overnight, then scoop it into the bin.

DIRECTIONS:

Scoop shea butter and beeswax into a microwave-safe bowl with a pourable spout. Microwave in 30-second increments at 50 per cent power, stirring each time, until mixture mostly liquefies. Remove bowl from microwave with oven gloves. Stir in coconut oil until clear, not cloudy. Let cool slightly, then add essential oil.

Create a tight seal at the bottom of an empty deodorant tube by screwing canister to its lowest setting. (Reuse a deodorant tube or buy an empty deodorant tube at an online speciality shop.) Over bin, carefully pour liquid into empty deodorant tube until full. Place cap on top and keep in refrigerator overnight until liquid solidifies.

Makes enough to fill an empty deodorant tube. Store in a cool, dry place. Use within 3–4 weeks.

Fresh Feet Spray

You will need:

4 tbsp apple cider vinegar
2 tbsp distilled water
6 drops tea tree essential oil

Smelly feet can be embarrassing, but this spray will help! Apple cider vinegar naturally absorbs smells and can help tame toenail fungus. Tea tree oil is known for deodorizing and healing too. Shake before each use.

apple cider vinegar

Tea Tree

DIRECTIONS:

Mix all ingredients in a small bowl with a pourable spout. Pour into a 90-ml spray bottle. Store in a cool, dry place. Use within 2 weeks.

Pedicure Slippers

After a pedicure, your nails need to dry before you can wear shoes. Make a pair of these foam slippers and you'll feel like you're at the salon. There's one difference: these slippers are a bit more glam! If you're having friends over for a pedicure party, make a few pairs in advance.

You will need:

30 x 46 cm piece of foam
scissors
pen
2 brads
3D flower stickers (optional)

DIRECTIONS:

Trace your feet or a pair of shoes onto a piece of foam. Now trace a second line 1.25 centimetres in from the outline of your feet. Cut along that outer line. On the inner line, draw a small X at the middle point of each side of foot. Puncture the foam with scissors at the left X and cut along the inner line and around the heel until you reach the right X.

Fold the recently cut end upwards and secure with a brad at the top, near where you want your big toe to fit. The brad should puncture the foam easily. Makes one pair of slippers. Decorate with 3D flower stickers, glitter, rhinestones or anything else you can think of to make your slippers stand out!

Tingly Salt Scrub for Feet

You will need:

270 g sea salt
120 ml olive oil
12 drops peppermint essential oil
12 drops tea tree essential oil

After a good scrub, your feet will feel soft and smooth! The peppermint and tea tree essential oils cause a cooling, tingling effect during the process. To use, massage a handful onto your feet while sitting over a bath or a large bowl of water with a towel underneath it. Rinse, then pat feet dry with a clean towel.

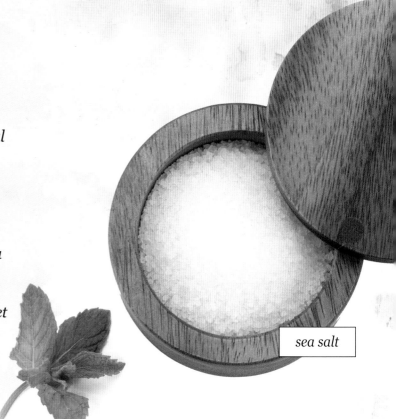

sea salt

Be careful! Oils and butters can make bath surfaces slippery. A non-slip bath mat may help. Wipe bath with a dry towel when finished.

DIRECTIONS:

Mix all ingredients in a small bowl. Scoop into a lidded glass container. Store in a cool, dry place. Use within 3–4 weeks.

Smelly Shoe Sachets

You will need:

220 g bicarbonate of soda
130 g cornstarch
½ tsp tea tree essential oil
2 long socks

The bicarbonate of soda and tea tree essential oil in this recipe will help absorb the odour in your favourite pair of shoes. To use, place sachets snugly into the toe of your shoe and let sit overnight or for a few days. Replace the ingredients every three months.

bicarbonate of soda

cornstarch

DIRECTIONS:

Mix all ingredients together in a bowl with a pouring spout. Pour half of mixture into each sock. (A funnel will help, and it's best to place each sock in a bowl to catch the mess.) Tie remaining length of sock tightly in a knot. Makes two sachets.

Body

Bathe in a refreshing tub tea, buff with your very own handmade shower puff and beautify with a lovely lotion. There's a recipe for everyone, from calming mixes for sensitive skin to moisturizing products that soothe dry, itchy patches to a dream-inducing lavender lotion that will help you to get your beauty rest.

sweet dreams cream

bath salts

shower steamers

Shower Puff

Scrub-a-dub-dub! These shower puffs are quick and simple to make, and they make great gifts too. Use a different colour netting in the centre to make an extra pretty puff, or add more layers for an extra fluffy version.

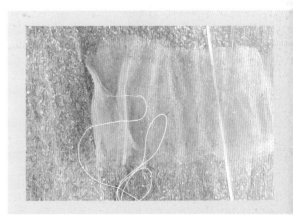

DIRECTIONS:

Cut the nylon netting into three strips that each measure 15 x 183 centimetres. Stack the layers, then secure stacks in place at top, bottom and centre with safety pins. Thread the needle, then knot end of floss to safety pin at bottom. Starting at bottom centre, sew a long running stitch, about 2.5 centimetres in length. Repeat along entire length of netting.

Remove safety pins from fabric, then grab each end of floss. Push netting towards centre. Tie ends of floss tightly in a double knot. The netting should now form a sphere. Trim ends. Secure a loop of cord through the centre and finish with a knot.

Vanilla Honey Shower Scrub

You will need:

225 g white sugar
60 ml olive oil
2 tbsp honey
½ tsp vanilla extract

sugar

Sugar scrubs aren't just for hands and feet – this one is for your full body! While showering, scoop a small amount into your hands. Rub it into your skin, then rinse well. Not only will you feel re-energized, but your shower will smell delicious!

Be careful! Oils and butters can make bath surfaces slippery. A non-slip bath mat may help. Wipe bath with a dry towel when finished.

DIRECTIONS:

Mix all ingredients in a small bowl. Store in a lidded glass container. Store in a cool, dry place.

Secret Solid Perfume

You will need:

- 2 tbsp grated beeswax or beeswax pastilles
- 2 tsp jojoba oil
- 10 drops Roman chamomile essential oil
- 4 drops orange essential oil
- 10 drops lavender essential oil

This solid perfume makes a great gift and is perfect for girls on the go. Reuse a miniature mint tin, a small jam jar or even a jewellery locket and keep it in your bag or pocket. No one will know what's really inside!

beeswax pastilles

Lavender

DIRECTIONS:

Scoop beeswax into a microwave-safe bowl with a pourable spout. Microwave in 30-second increments at 50 per cent power, stirring each time, until it mostly liquefies. Remove bowl with oven gloves and stir until clear, not cloudy. Add jojoba oil and essential oils and stir. Immediately pour into container of your choice. Let harden at room temperature. This recipe makes about 1 tablespoon. Store in a cool, dry place.

Tub Teas

These bags of tub tea are so simple to make and use. Store each organza bag in a resealable plastic bag in case they leak a bit – it's okay if they do! To use, fill bath with warm water, then place organza bag directly in water and let it soak for the duration of your bath. Remove the organza bag when done and dispose of the bag.

Calming Tub Tea

This fragrance-free mix is perfect for sensitive skin.

You will need:

7.5 x 10 cm organza bag
80 g oats
53 g powdered milk
63 g Epsom salts
1 tsp bicarbonate of soda

powdered milk

Re-energizing Tub Tea

A wake-me-up blend that energizes tired muscles.

You will need:

7.5 x 10 cm organza bag
80 g oats
125 g Epsom salts
65 g coarse sea salt
5 drops peppermint essential oil
10 drops lemon essential oil
10 drops orange essential oil

DIRECTIONS:

Blend oats in a food processor or blender. Mix all ingredients in a bowl with a pourable spout, then stir. Pour into organza bag and tie in a knot. Makes one bag.

Cinnamon Vanilla Whipped Body Butter

You will need:

105 g shea butter
60 ml coconut oil
½ tbsp jojoba oil
½ tsp ground cinnamon
½ tsp vanilla extract

This whipped body butter looks like luxurious lotion, and it will melt in your hands. Your skin will feel silky smooth, look like it's glowing and smell good too! Massage this into your skin before bed, so the lotion can work its magic all night. Remember, a little goes a long way.

jojoba oil

DIRECTIONS:

Scoop shea butter into a microwave-safe mixing bowl. Microwave in 30-second increments at 50 per cent power, stirring each time, until it mostly liquefies. Remove bowl with oven gloves. Stir in coconut oil until mixture is clear, not cloudy. Add jojoba oil and stir.

To turn the mixture into cream, cover bowl with cling film and let cool in refrigerator until the texture resembles softened butter (this step should take no longer than an hour). If mixture fully hardens, remove from refrigerator and let it warm on the worktop. Add cinnamon and vanilla, then whip with a hand mixer on low speed for 3–5 minutes or until the colour brightens and peaks form.

When desired consistency is reached, scoop into lidded glass jar with a spoon. Store in a cool, dry place.

Natural Shaving Cream

You will need:

70 g shea butter
80 ml coconut oil
2 tbsp olive oil

Make your own nourishing and natural lotion that protects your skin while you shave. This cream is thick and may clog your razor blade. Rinse blade under water after every few strokes. Clean the razor after each use by soaking it in a cup with washing-up liquid and hot water, then scrubbing it clean with an old toothbrush.

shea butter

Be careful! Oils and butters can make bath surfaces slippery. A non-slip bath mat may help. Wipe bath with a dry towel when finished.

DIRECTIONS:

Scoop shea butter into a microwave-safe mixing bowl. Microwave in 30-second increments at 50 per cent power, stirring each time, until it mostly liquefies. Remove bowl with oven gloves. Stir in coconut oil until mixture is clear, not cloudy. Add olive oil and stir.

To turn the mixture into cream, cover bowl with cling film and let cool in refrigerator until the texture resembles softened butter (this step should take no longer than an hour). If mixture fully hardens, remove from refrigerator and let it warm on the worktop. Whip with a hand mixer on low speed for 3–5 minutes or until the colour brightens and peaks form.

When desired consistency is reached, scoop into jar with spatula. Store in a cool, dry place.

Sweet Dreams Cream

You will need:

240 ml coconut oil
15 drops lavender essential oil
25 drops Roman chamomile
essential oil

Coconut oil is great for your skin. This whipped version makes it even easier to use. You can rub this sleep salve just about anywhere: your hands, your feet, even your temples. The lavender and chamomile will help lull you to dreamland. Remember, a little goes a long way.

Roman
Chamomile

DIRECTIONS:

Scoop the coconut oil into a mixing bowl. Does it look and feel like softened butter? Then it's ready to go! (If it's liquid, cover bowl with cling film and let harden in refrigerator until the texture resembles softened butter. This step should take no longer than an hour.) Add essential oil, then whip with a hand mixer on low speed for 3–5 minutes or until the colour brightens and peaks form.

When desired consistency is reached, scoop into jar with spatula. Store in a cool, dry place.

Bathing Beauty Melts

You will need:

240 ml shea butter
1 tbsp coconut oil
2 tbsp Epsom salts
55 g bicarbonate of soda
10 drops lavender essential oil (optional)
5 drops Roman chamomile essential oil (optional)
1 tbsp pink edible shimmer dust (optional)
silicone treat moulds

Transform your bath into a spa-like soak when you drop one of these bath melts inside. This recipe may be called "bathing beauty", but it will help lull you into "sleeping beauty" mode. Chamomile and lavender have a calming effect for the perfect bedtime mix, but these beauty melts are great without essential oils too.

Epsom salts

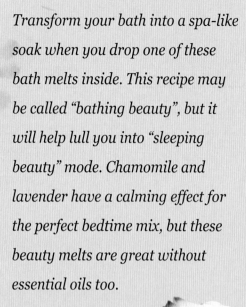

Be careful! Oils and butters can make bath surfaces slippery. A non-slip bath mat may help. Wipe bath with a dry towel when finished.

DIRECTIONS:

Melt the shea butter in 30-second increments at 50 per cent power in a microwave-safe bowl with a pourable spout. Carefully remove from microwave with oven gloves. Stir in coconut oil until melted.

Stir in Epsom salts, bicarbonate of soda, essential oils and shimmer dust. Pour mixture into silicone treat moulds and let harden at room temperature. Makes five or six medium-sized bath melts. Store individually in a cool, dry place.

Spa Towel Wrap

You will need:

- bath towel
- safety pins
- 30 cm of Velcro tape (2 cm in width)
- permanent fabric glue
- marker
- flannel of a different colour (optional)

It's the perfect blend between a towel and a robe! With a little bit of Velcro, this wrap stays in place, which means you can dry off hands free.

Optional: Cut shapes from a flannel of a different colour and glue them to the outside of the towel wrap as decoration. Let dry overnight.

DIRECTIONS:

With the top corner in each hand, hold a towel open and centered behind you. Wrap the left edge around the front of your body until it reaches your right armpit.

Make an X with a marker or masking tape on the corner nearest your right armpit and again near your left armpit.

Now wrap the right edge around the front of your body so it reaches your left armpit. Fold the excess material inwards and pin it in place.

Make two Xs on on the inside of the outer layer of the towel by simply mirroring the Xs you already made.

Remove the towel from your body and lay it flat on the ground with excess material facing up. Run a length of glue along the inside edges of excess material and press firmly. Remove safety pin.

Cut four 7.5-cm pieces of Velcro tape (two pieces of each kind). Glue the Velcro strips with scratchy sides to the Xs on this side of the towel. Flip over the towel, then glue the Velcro strips with fuzzy sides to the Xs. Let dry overnight.

Bath Salts

Soak your cares away. These bath salts turn any ordinary bath into a spa-like experience. To use, dissolve bath salts into warm water, then soak in the bath for 20 minutes. The salts in this recipe have great detoxifying benefits and can help relieve aches and pains. Choose the lavender version for its calming properties that relax your mind and your muscles, or pick peppermint for an invigorating soak.

Epsom salts

sea salt

Lovely Lavender Bath Salts

You will need:

270 g sea salt
250 g Epsom salts
10 drops lavender essential oil
2–3 drops purple food
   colouring (optional)

Peppermint Bath Salts

You will need:

270 g sea salt
250 g Epsom salts
10 drops peppermint essential oil
2–3 drops green food colouring
   (optional)

DIRECTIONS:

Pour the salts into a lidded glass container. Add essential oil, then food colouring. Stir all ingredients together. Makes enough for two soaks. Store extra for up to 2 weeks in a cool, dry place.

Mocha Salt Scrub

You will need:

- 135 g coarse sea salt
- 20 g ground coffee
- 60 ml olive oil
- 1 tbsp cocoa powder
- ½ tsp vanilla extract

Here's an energizing body scrub that will wake you up! The coffee and salt exfoliate your skin so you're ready to take on the day feeling fresh and clean. Plus, it turns out cocoa powder isn't just for baking – it's great for your skin too. To use, massage a small handful onto your body.

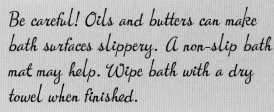

Be careful! Oils and butters can make bath surfaces slippery. A non-slip bath mat may help. Wipe bath with a dry towel when finished.

DIRECTIONS:

Mix all ingredients in a bowl. Stir together, then scoop into a lidded jar. Store in a cool, dry place.

Shower Steamers

Aromatherapy is the use of essential oils in bath products to help balance mind, body and spirit. These shower steamers smell great, thanks to a blend of essential oils that release into the air as you shower. To use, wet a steamer in your shower and place it on a ledge. Depending on the size of your steamers, you may want to use more than one at a time.

Good Night Shower Steamers

This is a relaxing blend that calms your mind and your body.

You will need:

220 g bicarbonate of soda
120 ml citric acid
1 tbsp witch hazel in spray bottle
5 drops lavender essential oil
10 drops Roman chamomile essential oil
5 drops orange essential oil
silicone mould
rubber gloves

Good Morning Shower Steamers

A happy, energizing mix to wake you up and put a smile on your face.

You will need:

220 g bicarbonate of soda
120 ml citric acid
1 tbsp witch hazel in spray bottle
5 drops peppermint essential oil
10 drops lemon essential oil
10 drops orange essential oil
silicone mould
rubber gloves

Be careful! Wear gloves when making this recipe. Citric acid could irritate your skin or eyes.

Tip: If the scent wears off, apply a few drops of essential oil directly to each shower steamer before using.

DIRECTIONS:

In a large bowl, combine the bicarbonate of soda and citric acid. Stir until smooth and all lumps are removed. Add essential oils and stir. Spritz mixture with 5–10 sprays of witch hazel, then mix with your hands (don't forget the gloves!).

Continue until mixture is slightly damp, but not wet enough to form a ball. Use as little witch hazel as possible, otherwise the shower steamers will expand as they dry.

When the mixture reaches the desired texture, press it firmly into silicone moulds. Let dry overnight. Remove carefully from moulds, then store in a resealable plastic bag or glass jar. Makes about 5 small shower steamers.

Luxurious Lotion Bars

You will need:

120 ml coconut oil
105 g shea butter
115 g grated beeswax or
    beeswax pastilles
20 drops Roman chamomile
    essential oil (optional)
silicone treat mould

These lotion bars are great for travelling. Although they're solid, the warmth from your hands allows them to easily melt into a luxurious cream exactly when you need it. They make great gifts too!

DIRECTIONS:

Scoop shea butter and beeswax into a microwave-safe bowl with a pourable spout. Microwave in 30-second increments at 50 per cent power, stirring each time, until mixture mostly liquefies. Remove bowl with oven gloves. Stir in coconut oil until clear, not cloudy. Let cool slightly, then add essential oil.

Using oven gloves, carefully pour liquid into silicone moulds. Let harden overnight at room temperature, then remove carefully from mould. Store in an airtight container in a cool, dry place.

Bugs-Be-Gone Spray

You will need:

3 tbsp witch hazel
2 tbsp distilled water
½ tsp vegetable glycerine
15 drops tea tree essential oil
5 drops lavender essential oil

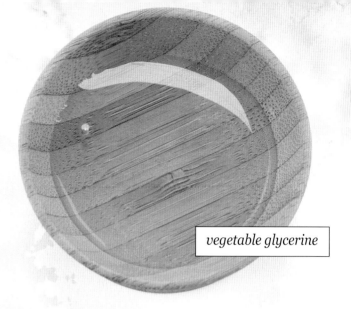

Keep the bugs at bay with a natural spray. Tea tree oil and lavender are said to help repel mosquitoes, while witch hazel can reduce that itchy feeling that accompanies a nasty bite. To use, spritz onto exposed skin before going outside. Avoid contact with your eyes.

vegetable glycerine

Be careful! If spray stings, wash it from your skin immediately.

DIRECTIONS:

Mix ingredients in a glass bowl with a pourable spout.
Pour into a 60-ml spray bottle.

DIY Deodorant

You can whip up this natural alternative at home. This is a deodorant, so it will prevent body odour. However, it is not an antiperspirant, so it won't prevent sweating. Depending on what you believe, that may be a good thing; some people argue that sweating is good for your body.

You will need:

120 ml coconut oil
30 g cornstarch
55 g bicarbonate of soda
15 drops tea tree essential oil

DIRECTIONS:

Scoop coconut oil into a microwave-safe bowl with pourable spout. Microwave in 10-second increments at 50 per cent power, stirring each time, until it mostly liquefies. Remove bowl with oven gloves and stir until clear, not cloudy. Let cool slightly, then stir in additional ingredients.

Create a tight seal at the bottom of an empty deodorant tube by screwing canister to its lowest setting. (Reuse a deodorant tube or buy an empty deodorant tube at an online speciality shop.) Wearing an oven glove to protect your hand, hold the deodorant tube over a bin. Then carefully pour liquid into empty tube until full. Place cap on top and keep in refrigerator overnight until liquid solidifies.

DIY Deodorant for Sensitive Skin

If the above recipe is too harsh on your skin, it may be because of the bicarbonate of soda. This recipe lessens the bicarbonate of soda and replaces it with soothing shea butter, which should help alleviate some skin sensitivities.

You will need:

80 ml coconut oil

75 g grated beeswax or beeswax pastilles

40 g cornstarch

3 tbsp shea butter

2 tbsp bicarbonate of soda

15 drops tea tree essential oil

DIRECTIONS:

Scoop beeswax and shea butter into a microwave-safe bowl with pourable spout. Microwave in 30-second increments at 50 per cent power, stirring each time, until mixture mostly liquefies. Remove bowl with oven gloves. Stir in coconut oil until mixture is clear, not cloudy. Let cool slightly, then stir in additional ingredients.

Create a tight seal at the bottom of an empty deodorant tube by screwing canister to its lowest setting. (Reuse a deodorant tube or buy an empty deodorant tube at an online speciality shop.) Wearing an oven glove to protect your hand, hold the deodorant tube over a bin. Then carefully pour liquid into empty tube until full. Place cap on top and keep in refrigerator overnight until liquid solidifies.

Face

Face it – skin on your face needs to be taken care of differently from the skin on the rest of your body. It's more delicate and comes with its own set of problems such as acne, clogged pores and dry or oily patches. These recipes will help balance your skin in a natural way. And don't worry, we didn't forget about your teeth. After all, your smile is the most important part of your face!

rosewater toner

vanilla coffee lip scrub

exfoliating face scrub

Chocolate Mousse Face Mask

You will need:

1 tbsp honey
2 tsp cocoa powder
1 tsp jojoba oil or olive oil
¼ tsp fine sea salt

Would you like to order off the dessert menu? This cleansing chocolate mask will soothe breakouts, and it acts as a gentle exfoliating scrub when you rinse it off. To use, gently massage a thin layer onto face, avoiding eye area. Leave on for 10 minutes, then rinse off mask completely before patting face dry with a clean towel.

cocoa powder

Be careful! If a face mask stings, wash it from your skin immediately.

DIRECTIONS:

Mix all ingredients together in a bowl. Stir until mixture forms a pudding-like paste. This recipe makes one mask.

Breakfast Face Mask

You will need:

- 1 tsp powdered milk
- 1 tsp honey
- 3 tsp plain yoghurt

You can eat your breakfast and wear it too! This mask combines milk, honey and yoghurt to form a calming and cooling mask you'll love. To use, gently massage a thick layer onto face, avoiding eye area. Leave on for 10 minutes, then rinse off mask completely before patting face dry with a clean towel.

yoghurt

powdered milk

Be careful! If any face mask ever stings, wash it from your skin immediately.

DIRECTIONS:

Mix powdered milk, honey and yoghurt in a small bowl. Stir until mixture forms a paste. This recipe makes one mask.

Rosewater Toner

You will need:

60 ml rosewater
2 tbsp witch hazel
¼ tsp vegetable glycerine

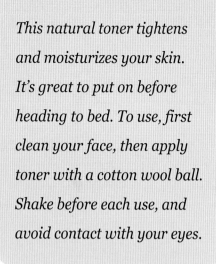

This natural toner tightens and moisturizes your skin. It's great to put on before heading to bed. To use, first clean your face, then apply toner with a cotton wool ball. Shake before each use, and avoid contact with your eyes.

vegetable glycerine

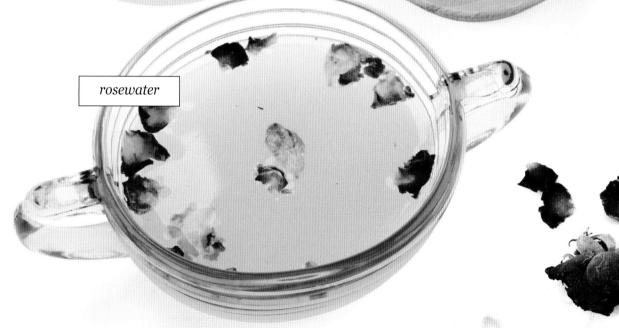

rosewater

DIRECTIONS:

Mix ingredients in a bowl with a pourable spout. Pour mixture into a lidded container. Makes enough to fill a 60-ml bottle.

Cooling Facial Refresher Spray

You will need:

60 ml aloe vera gel
5 drops peppermint essential oil
¼ tsp witch hazel

Aloe vera gel and peppermint essential oil create a cooling effect, which can provide temporary relief from sunburns or hot days. Shake before use, and avoid contact with your eyes by covering them with your hand or a flannel. Store in the refrigerator to keep spray extra cool.

aloe vera gel

DIRECTIONS:

Mix all ingredients in a bowl with a pourable spout. Pour into a 60-ml spray bottle.

Eye Pillow

The lavender in this mask has a calming effect, and the cooling sensation can help soothe puffy eyes. Place in the freezer for a few hours, then rest the pillow across your eyes for 15 minutes. It can also be warmed in the microwave* for 30 seconds. Make a few extra to share with friends!

DIRECTIONS:

Pour rice into a bowl with a pourable spout. Add essential oil and stir. Before you pour the mixture into the sock, tie a knot at the toe end of the sock. Then pour the rice mixture into the sock while holding sock over a bowl to catch any spills. Leave about 7.5 centimetres of sock on the end. Then form a knot, and pull tightly. Replace rice and lavender oil every six months – or sooner if the fragrance begins to fade.

* If you microwave the eye mask, make sure you check the temperature of it with the back of your hand before putting it on your eyes.

Vanilla Coffee Lip Scrub

You will need:

57 g white sugar
1 tsp ground coffee
1 tbsp olive oil
1 tsp vanilla extract

Chapped lips? No problem! A good scrub can flake away any dead skin and reveal your healthy lips. While standing over a sink, use your finger to scoop out a small amount of the scrub, then rub it onto your lips in a circular motion. Rinse off excess. This makes your lips feel great, and it tastes good too!

sugar

DIRECTIONS:

Mix the ingredients together in a small bowl. Scoop a portion into a small, clear, circular storage container with screw-top lid. This recipe makes about five portions.

Coconut Lip Balm

You will need:

2 tbsp coconut oil
2 tbsp grated beeswax or
   beeswax pastilles
4 tsp olive oil

Making lip balm is easier than you might think. Coconut oil and olive oil can serve as natural lip healing remedies on their own, but we're going to mix them together to create a nourishing blend.

coconut oil

beeswax pastilles

DIRECTIONS:

Scoop beeswax and coconut oil into a microwave-safe bowl with a pourable spout. Microwave in 30-second increments at 50 per cent power, stirring each time, until mixture mostly liquefies. Remove bowl with oven gloves and stir until clear, not cloudy. Add olive oil and stir.

Carefully pour into small, clear, circular storage containers with screw-top lids. Let harden at room temperature, then screw on caps. This recipe makes about six lip balms.

Warming Lemon Honey Face Wash

You will need:

- 3 tbsp honey
- 3 tbsp vegetable glycerine
- 3 drops lemon essential oil

Sensitive skin? This natural face wash smells sweet and will keep your skin looking bright and soft while fighting off acne. Honey is antibacterial, which means it's a great cleanser, and it helps to heal your skin. This face wash won't produce suds, but don't worry – it's working! To use, massage a small amount in circular motions gently onto your dry face. It will warm naturally as you rub it onto your skin. Rinse with warm water, then pat dry with a clean towel.

Tip: Raw unfiltered honey can be found at natural food shops and may have more benefits for your skin than processed honey.

DIRECTIONS:

Stir all ingredients in a bowl with a pourable spout. Pour into a plastic squeeze bottle or tube. This recipe makes enough to fill a 90-ml bottle.

Skin-Soothing Spray

You will need:

2 tbsp aloe vera gel
4 tbsp rosewater
3 drops Roman chamomile essential oil
   (optional)

Hydrate and soften your skin with this ultra-calming spray that smells good too. Shake before each use, and avoid contact with your eyes by covering them with your hand or a flannel.

aloe vera gel

DIRECTIONS:

Mix all ingredients in a bowl with a pourable spout. Pour into a glass spray bottle. This recipe makes enough to fill a 60-ml spray bottle.

Exfoliating Face Scrub

You will need:

3 tsp bicarbonate of soda
2 tsp jojoba oil

Give your skin a gentle scrub with this bicarbonate of soda-based mix. To use, massage a small amount in circular motions gently onto your dry face. Rinse with warm water, then pat dry with a clean towel.

jojoba oil

DIRECTIONS:

Mix all ingredients in a small bowl. This recipe makes enough for a single use.

DIY Scented Sprays

Sometimes a whiff of a sweet scent can make you instantly feel better! These sprays will help to energize or calm you throughout the day. They also can be great gifts to give to friends.

Dreamy Pillow Mist

To be at your best, you need your beauty sleep! This pillow mist will help lull you to dreamland thanks to a calming blend of lavender and chamomile. Shake before each use.

Citrus Linen Spray

With a spritz of this linen spray, your sheets will smell fresh and clean thanks to the lemon scent, which is deodorizing and energizing. This can be used as a room spray too, and it's especially perfect for early mornings. Shake before each use.

You will need:

3 tbsp distilled water
1 tsp witch hazel
15 drops lemon essential oil

DIRECTIONS:

Mix all ingredients in a bowl with a pourable spout. Pour into a spray bottle. Each recipe makes enough to fill a 60-ml container.

Face Lotions

The ingredients in these recipes have low comedogenic ratings, which means they are less likely to clog your pores. Shea butter and jojoba oil might feel greasy, but both ingredients are exceptional ways to nourish, moisturize and heal your skin. To use, massage a small amount onto your face and neck. Remember, a little goes a long way!

Calming Face Lotion

This lotion will soothe your skin as well as soothe your mind thanks to the calming scent.

You will need:

55 g shea butter
4 tbsp jojoba oil
10–15 drops lavender essential oil

Acne-Fighting Face Lotion

This lotion will moisturize while healing and preventing acne – without drying out your skin.

You will need:

55 g shea butter
4 tbsp jojoba oil
10–15 drops tea tree essential oil

DIRECTIONS:

Scoop shea butter into a microwave-safe mixing bowl. Microwave in 30-second increments at 50 per cent power, stirring each time, until it mostly liquefies. Remove bowl with oven gloves and stir until clear, not cloudy. Add jojoba oil and stir.

To turn the liquid into a cream, cover the bowl with cling film and place in the refrigerator until the texture resembles softened butter (this step should take no longer than one hour). Add essential oil, then whip with a hand mixer on low speed for 3–5 minutes or until the colour brightens and peaks form.

When desired consistency is reached, scoop into a lidded glass jar with a spatula.

Soothing Face Wipes

You will need:
extra virgin olive oil
cotton wool pads
   (make-up remover pads)
small jar

Olive oil is a safe and easy way to get your face squeaky clean – it even removes make-up, including mascara. Olive oil moisturizes your skin as it cleans, and it will leave your face feeling incredibly smooth. To use, gently massage the wipe across your face and neck. Rinse with warm water, then pat dry.

olive oil

DIRECTIONS:

Stack seven cotton wool pads in a small jar. Pour a small amount of olive oil into the jar, covering each cotton wool pad. The cotton wool pads should be damp, not soaked. This recipe makes enough face wipes for 1 week.

Minty Homemade Toothpaste

You will need:

80 ml coconut oil

73 g bicarbonate of soda

¼ tsp Stevia extract powder
for sweetness (optional)

10 drops peppermint essential oil

To use, scoop a small amount of paste onto your toothbrush. The paste will melt in your mouth as you brush. Brush your teeth for two minutes, then spit and rinse. Do not swallow the toothpaste.

coconut oil

bicarbonate of soda

DIRECTIONS:

Melt coconut oil in microwavable-safe bowl in 10-second increments at 50 per cent power, stirring in between. Remove from microwave with oven gloves. Stir in bicarbonate of soda and Stevia.

To turn the liquid into a paste, cover the bowl with cling film and place in the refrigerator until the liquid resembles softened butter (this step should take no longer than one hour). Add essential oil, then whip with a hand mixer on low speed for 3–5 minutes, or until the colour brightens and peaks form. Store in a cool, dry place.

Peppermint Mouthwash

You will need:

4 tbsp distilled water
¼ tsp bicarbonate of soda
⅛ tsp salt
⅛ tsp Stevia extract powder for
  sweetness (optional)
1–2 drops peppermint essential oil

If you wear braces, it can be hard to clean your teeth completely. Mouthwashes can help! Shake bottle before each use, then pour a small amount into a cup. Swish in your mouth for 30 seconds, then spit into sink. Do not swallow.

salt

Peppermint

DIRECTIONS:

Mix all ingredients in a bowl with a pourable spout. Pour into a lidded bottle. Makes enough to fill a 60-ml bottle. Store in a cool, dry place.

Hair

Our hair takes on a lot of stress. It gets blown around, twisted up, pulled back, curled, straightened, dyed and more. Treat your hair right with these nourishing recipes. We'll take on tangles, frizz and dull hair with everything from dry shampoos to sprays to masks. We'll also give your hair some flair, with DIY projects for headbands, decorative hair grips and more.

deep conditioning treatment

hair spray

twisted headband

Creaseless Hair Tie

It's super easy to make your own fancy hair ties. All you need is fold-over elastic, which is a soft, stretchy ribbon that can be found in the sewing aisle of craft shops. It comes in lots of fun colours and patterns.

DIRECTIONS:

Cut a 25-centimetre long piece of fold-over elastic. Fold it in half lengthwise, then tie the ends together into a knot. Pull tightly to secure. Line the raw edges with a thin line of clear nail polish to prevent fraying. Let dry overnight.

Ribbon Headband

You will need:

hair band
3 colours of ribbon
tape measure
scissors

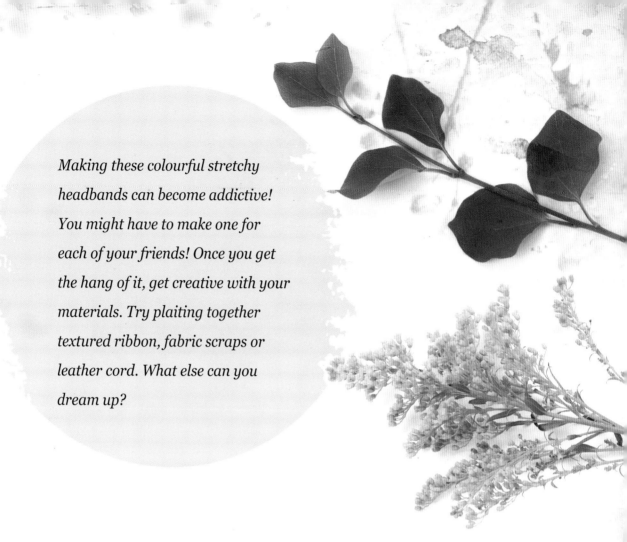

Making these colourful stretchy headbands can become addictive! You might have to make one for each of your friends! Once you get the hang of it, get creative with your materials. Try plaiting together textured ribbon, fabric scraps or leather cord. What else can you dream up?

DIRECTIONS:

With a tape measure, measure around your head as if you were wearing an elastic headband. Add 15 centimetres to that measurement. Now cut three ribbons to that length. Knot one end to a hair band by stacking the three ribbons, then threading the ends through the centre of the hair band and back around to form a loop. Push the ends of the ribbon through the loop and pull tightly.

Hook the hair band onto a doorknob or cabinet knob and begin plaiting the ribbon. When about 7.5 centimetres remain, knot the remaining ribbon onto the hair band following the same directions above. Pull tightly and trim ends.

Spa Hair Wrap

You will need:

76 x 137 cm bath towel (or two
    40 x 71 cm hand towels)
fabric marker
scissors
fold-over elastic (15 mm in width)
fabric glue

Have you ever wrapped your hair up in a towel only to have the towel fall off your head? This craft turns a towel (a thin one works best) into a perfectly sized wrap that will help your hair dry quickly.

Tip: Pick out a towel with a bold colour or pattern, or add your own designs with a fabric marker.

DIRECTIONS:

If using a bath towel, fold it in half lengthwise. If using two hand towels, stack them on top of each other. Draw the shape shown in the bottom left image on your towel with a fabric marker. Use the finished seam as the bottom of the pattern. It should measure 64 centimetres long and be 25 centimetres high at its highest point. Cut out pattern when done.

Remove top layer and set aside. Cut a 10-centimetre piece of fold-over elastic and fold it in half. Glue the ends together so it forms a loop. Then glue the loop to the left edge of your towel, about 10 centimetres from the bottom seam.

On the bottom layer of fabric, glue a line about 15 millimetres in from the edge, leaving the finished bottom edge unglued. Place the second layer of towel on top and press firmly along the glued edges. Let dry overnight. When dry, turn the towel inside out.

Deep Conditioning Treatment

You will need:

6 tbsp coconut oil
4 tbsp shea butter
2 tsp jojoba oil

Give your hair the ultimate conditioning treatment. The oils and butters in this recipe can work wonders on dry hair. To use, massage a very small amount into damp hair. Leave on for 10 minutes, then shampoo and condition as usual. This balm can also be used sparingly as a leave-in conditioner on the ends of dry hair. Massage mixture into your hands first, then rub hands along ends of hair.

shea butter

DIRECTIONS:

Scoop shea butter into a microwave-safe bowl with a pourable spout. Microwave in 30-second increments at 50 per cent power, stirring each time, until it mostly liquefies. Remove bowl with oven gloves. Stir in coconut oil until mixture is clear, not cloudy. Add jojoba oil and stir. Pour into a 120-ml jar. Let sit overnight so oils and butter can cool to form a cream.

Dry Shampoo

Greasy hair? No problem! Dry shampoo can give your hair a pick-me-up when you don't have time to wash it. Use a spice jar so you can easily sprinkle this powder onto your hair, or dip a make-up brush in a jar and brush the powder onto your hair. Apply the powder sparingly to greasy sections of hair.

cornstarch

cocoa powder

For light hair

You will need:

30 g cornstarch
1 tbsp bicarbonate of soda
2 drops lavender essential oil
(optional)

For dark hair

You will need:

2 tbsp cornstarch
2 tbsp unsweetened cocoa
powder
1 tsp bicarbonate of soda
2 drops peppermint essential oil
(optional)

DIRECTIONS:

Combine all ingredients in a bowl and stir. Scoop into container.
Makes enough to fill a 90-ml spice jar.

Surf Spray

You will need:

- 3 tbsp aloe vera gel
- 1 tbsp distilled water
- 2 tsp fine sea salt

Get beachy waves with this salt spray gel. To use, spray lightly onto slightly damp hair, then scrunch your locks! The salt in the spray can help to form waves that will make you look like you just got back from a dip in the ocean.

sea salt

Be careful! Sea salt sprays can damage hair if used too often, because salt has a drying effect. Make sure you condition your hair after using this spray.

DIRECTIONS:

Mix ingredients in a bowl with a pourable spout.
Pour into a 60-ml spray bottle.

125

Tame Those Tangles Spray

You will need:

3 tbsp apple cider vinegar

3 tbsp distilled water

15 drops lavender essential oil
  (optional)

Here's a recipe that will not only tame your tangles, but also leave your hair with a nice shine. The lavender essential oil will help to mask the strong smell of vinegar. To use, apply to damp hair (focusing on tangles), then brush through hair. Shake before each use.

DIRECTIONS:

Mix all ingredients in glass bowl with pourable spout.
Pour into a 60-ml reusable spray bottle.

Hair Spray

You will need:

1 tsp sugar
240 ml water (boiled)
3 drops lavender essential oil
(optional)

This spray will hold your hair in place, and it has a sweet aroma too. If the recipe below is too light of a hold for your hair, increase the sugar by 1 teaspoon until you reach the hold you'd like. Do not exceed 3 teaspoons.

DIRECTIONS:

Lightly boil water. Stir in sugar until water is clear, not cloudy. Remove from heat and let cool. Pour into glass bowl with pourable spout. Add essential oil and stir. Pour into container. Makes enough for two 60-ml spray bottles.

Hair Perfume Spray

You will need:

5 tbsp rosewater
1 tbsp aloe vera gel
5 drops Roman chamomile essential oil
2 drops orange essential oil
5 drops lavender essential oil

We love this recipe because it makes your hair smell like a summer breeze, and it also acts as a nourishing leave-in conditioner. Spray on wet hair straight after a shower or spray onto dry hair that needs a bit of a pick-me-up. Shake before each use.

Be careful! Close your eyes when using this spray.

DIRECTIONS:

Mix all ingredients in a bowl with a pourable spout. Pour into a 60-ml spray bottle.

Beautiful Hair Clips

Give your boring hair grips a makeover! This simple craft takes just a few minutes and uses nail polish as decorative paint. These pins can be customized for any holiday or season, and they make great gifts too.

You will need:

hair grips
nail polish
baking parchment
cardboard

DIRECTIONS:

Stack baking parchment on top of cardboard. Then slip the hair grips onto the stacked cardboard and paper. Make sure the hair grips are spaced out evenly. Lay a second sheet of baking parchment under the cardboard to protect your surface. Paint each hair grip with a layer of nail polish. Let dry, then add a second layer. Use a toothpick to add polka dots or stripes. Let dry overnight, then remove the grips from cardboard.

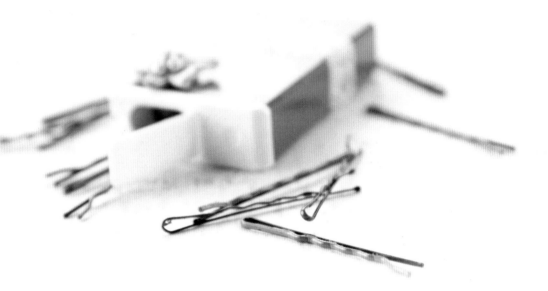

Hair Clip Case

You can never have enough hair grips! They always seem to disappear. But now that your hair grips are no longer boring, you won't want to lose them. Keep them organized in this cute case.

You will need:

empty plastic box
nail polish
baking parchment
ribbon (optional)
stickers (optional)

DIRECTIONS:

Protect your surface with a sheet of baking parchment. Now begin painting your plastic box with nail polish. Try polka dots, stripes or paint splatters. Let dry overnight, then fill it with your beautiful hair grips! Finish the case with ribbon or stickers, if you'd like.

Glam Twisted Headband

You will need:

pair of tights
scissors
hair tie

Turn an old pair of tights into a super cute hair wrap with a fashionable knot in front. The stretch in the tights and the stretch of a hair band ensure this wrap fits snugly around your head.

DIRECTIONS:

Cut the leg portions off of a pair of tights. Lay one leg horizontally on your surface and the next leg vertically on top of it to form a cross. Fold over the left side to the right side and the top to the bottom. Grab the ends of each side and pull until the lengths are even. Thread each end of the tights through the centre of the hair band and knot the ends around the band. Trim any excess material.

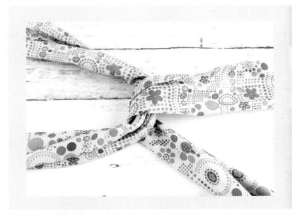

Hair Masks

With one of these nourishing hair masks, your locks will soon look and feel lovelier than ever! To use, apply evenly to your hair, then place a shower cap (or cling film) over your hair. Leave the mask on for 10 minutes, then rinse it out in the shower. Shampoo and condition as usual.

No More Frizz Mask

Strengthen your hair and reduce frizz at the same time with this nourishing mask.

You will need:

- 1 ripe banana
- 65 g plain yoghurt, or more for longer hair
- 1 tbsp honey

DIRECTIONS:

Put banana and yoghurt in a bowl and mix and mash together with a fork. Add honey and stir until blended well. Makes one mask.

Itchy Scalp Mask

If your scalp is feeling dry and you're fighting dandruff, give this moisturizing mask a try.

You will need:

- ½ ripe avocado
- 60 g mayonnaise, or more for longer hair
- 1 tbsp olive oil

DIRECTIONS:

Put avocado and mayonnaise in a bowl and mix and mash together with a fork. Add olive oil and stir until blended well. Makes one mask.

137

Smoothing Spray

You will need:

2 tbsp aloe vera gel
2 tbsp distilled water
1 tsp vegetable glycerine

Got frizz? Get rid of it! The aloe vera gel and glycerine in this recipe can help to tame unruly manes. A few spritzes of this spray go a long way. Spray lightly on dry hair, then brush through. Shake before each use.

aloe vera gel

DIRECTIONS:

Mix all ingredients in a bowl with a pourable spout.
Pour into 60-ml spray bottle.

Boho Hair Wrap

Give your hair a burst of temporary colour with embroidery floss. You can even add charms, feathers or beads if you dare! These wraps can be washed as usual in the shower but should be removed after two weeks. Or make your hair wrap removable by knotting the centre of the embroidery floss to the end of a hair grip (instead of the top of a plaited piece of hair). Then follow the directions in the second paragraph below.

Tip: Try crisscrossing colours, looping the floss to create a friendship bracelet effect, or leave segments of your plait showing. Make an ombre effect by picking three shades of one colour, then wrapping from light to dark or dark to light.

DIRECTIONS:

First, plait the piece of hair you'd like to wrap. Place a hair grip at the end to temporarily secure it. Cut three colours of embroidery floss three times the length of your plait and gather them together. Tie the centre of the embroidery floss in a tight knot at the top of the plait. Now six strings will hang loose.

Choose one piece of floss and start wrapping it around your hair, plus the other five pieces of floss. After about 2.5 centimetres, choose a different colour floss and begin wrapping it around your hair and the other five pieces of floss. It doesn't have to be perfect. When you're finished, tie the strings in a double knot.

Shimmer Hair Gel

A little shimmer never hurt anyone. Different colours can make any hairdo extra festive. To use, dip fingers in jar and apply gel to hair. If this hold isn't strong enough for your hair, try making it with 1 teaspoon of gelatin.

DIRECTIONS:

Boil 240 ml of water. Add gelatin and stir until dissolved. Let cool. Using a funnel or a bowl with a pourable spout, pour into container. Let set in refrigerator overnight. Once gel has set, stir in glitter. This gel must be stored in the refrigerator when not in use.

Treat yourself
(or someone else!)

This is the ultimate spa treatment! Learn how to package your lotions, sprays and more, how to have a relaxing at-home mani-pedi and how to decorate your new spa products so they look as beautiful as they make you feel!

lip care kit

HELLO FRIEND

sugar scrub trio

spa sprays

Manicures are about more than just the polish! Here's how you can pamper yourself pre- and post-manicure, and pull off a polish job that looks professional!

Start with the Chocolate Sugar Hand Scrub (page 16) or the Sea Salt Hand Scrub (page 26) to prep your hands and make them extra smooth. Once you've rinsed and dried your hands, finish by rubbing a thin layer of Cooling Peppermint Hand Cream (page 21) from your fingertips to your elbows.

sea salt hand scrub

Now begin painting your fingernails with a thin layer of polish. Try to do only three strokes on each nail – one stroke on the left side, one on the right and then one down the centre. That's it! Once you've completed one layer, go back and paint another thin layer on each fingernail. If you accidentally get nail polish on your skin, dip a small paintbrush or a cotton bud into a bottle of nail polish remover and carefully remove the mistake.

One way to make nails dry faster is to hold them under cold running water for 10 seconds. Try it! Once the polish is completely dry, finish with the Nail-Strengthening Serum (page 22) and rub it gently around the cuticles and on top of your nail. It will keep your nails and skin moisturized and can help to prevent your polish from getting chipped.

Your feet deserve just as much love as your hands. Here's the best way to prep for a perfect pedicure.

For pedicures, you'll be more comfortable in shorts or trousers that easily roll up to the knee. Start by exfoliating your feet with the Gingerbread Foot Scrub (page 34). Once your feet are scrubbed and patted dry, immerse them in the Soothing Soak for Tired Toes (page 33). Relaxing!

Pat your feet dry, then rub in the Cooling Sore Muscle Butter (page 36) from your toes to your knees. Now step into your foam Pedicure Slippers (page 42). It's time to start painting!

gingerbread foot scrub

foot soak

sore muscle butter

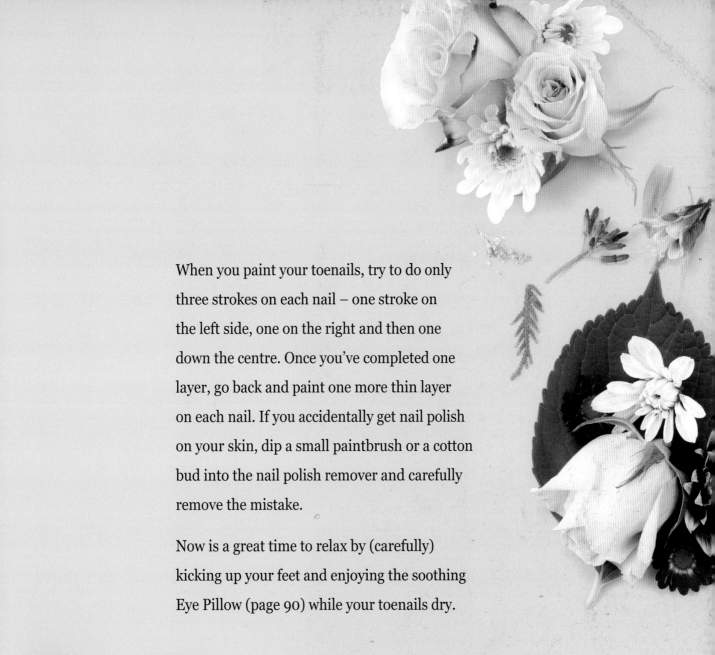

When you paint your toenails, try to do only three strokes on each nail – one stroke on the left side, one on the right and then one down the centre. Once you've completed one layer, go back and paint one more thin layer on each nail. If you accidentally get nail polish on your skin, dip a small paintbrush or a cotton bud into the nail polish remover and carefully remove the mistake.

Now is a great time to relax by (carefully) kicking up your feet and enjoying the soothing Eye Pillow (page 90) while your toenails dry.

eye pillow

PRETTY PACKAGING

All of your lotions, potions and sprays look and smell amazing, but as they're homemade, the jars they're in are often boring. Not only will these labelling ideas help to beautify your beauty products, they'll help you to remember what's what!

Simple stickers

Use letter stickers (found at craft shops) to spell out what's inside. Letter stickers come in all shapes and sizes, including glitter versions, so mix and match to create a unique look for each product.

Lovely labels

Adhesive sticker paper, which you can find in office supply shops, is the easiest way to make great labels in all sizes. Design a logo or a label on your computer and print it out on adhesive paper, or just draw your own directly on the adhesive paper with coloured pens or markers. Cut out your designs when you're finished and attach to the front or the lid of your product.

Top it off

If you're using mason jars to store your products, the top screws off in two pieces. Trace the circle portion onto a piece of paper. Write your product name with markers or stickers. Cut out and apply to lid with double-sided tape. Patterned washi tape can be applied to the edge of the screw portion to finish the look.

Gift Wrap: Nail Polish Marbling

You will need:

baking parchment
disposable plastic food container or bowl
water
4 bottles of nail polish
toothpick
grosgrain or satin ribbon of any width or length
paper gift tags

Decorating ribbons and tags with a beautiful marbling effect is a lot easier than it looks! A mix of nail polish and water is the perfect paint to brighten up plain wrapping. Four different bold or metallic jewel tones mix together best to form a pretty marbling pattern. As soon as the nail polish hits the water, it will begin to dry, so make sure you set up your supplies ahead of time and work fast.

Tip: Make your own gift tags! Trace the bottom of a jar or glass onto a piece of card stock, then cut out the circle. Use as is or add a hole at the top centre with a hole punch. Loop ribbon through the hole.

DIRECTIONS:

Line your surface with baking parchment. It will act as a space for your finished pieces to dry and will protect the surface from any spills. Now fill a shallow disposable plastic food container with two centimetres of water. Pour a few drops of each colour of nail polish into the bowl. Swirl colours with a toothpick.

Now grab each end of a ribbon length and place it along the surface of the water (keep the ends of the ribbon and your fingers out of the water). The nail polish pattern will imprint onto the ribbon like a stamp. Remove ribbon and place on the baking parchment to dry. Repeat with more ribbon or gift tags. For gift tags, immerse only half the tag in the mixture to avoid getting your hands wet.

To clean up, run a toothpick through the water to gather remaining nail polish (it will clump together). Throw it away. Pour water carefully down the sink, then dispose of the container or save it for a future marbling craft.

Gift Idea: Hair Flair

The Beautiful Hair Clips (page 132) and the Creaseless Hair Ties (page 114) are quick and easy gifts that everyone loves. Here's a super cute way to package these handmade crafts!

You will need:

jar
card stock
scissors
glitter
glue
coloured marker

Glittery Hair Clip Carrier

Trace the bottom of a jar onto back of card stock and cut along lines. Decorate the front side of card stock with glitter. Let glue dry before sliding decorated hair grips onto the circle.

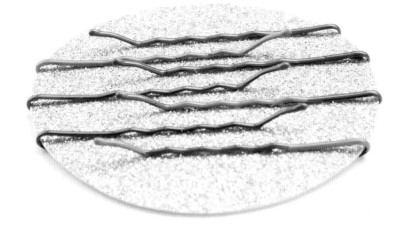

Hair Ties

Cut a 12.5 x 10 centimetre rectangle from plain card stock. Slide a few hair ties onto plain card stock. (If hair ties don't slide easily onto card stock, trim the card stock to be slimmer than 10 centimetres until hair ties fit.) If you want to add some flair, write a message with marker in between each hair tie.

Gift Idea: Spa Samples

You can really show off your handmade beauty skills when you create little gift sets that feature multiple products. Below are just a few ideas, but feel free to use your imagination and pair up the most perfect products for each person.

Spa Sprays

The Dreamy Pillow Mist (page 103), Hair Perfume Spray (page 130) and Cooling Facial Refresher Spray (page 88) make an especially soothing trio. Make sure each bottle is clearly labelled before giving away as a gift. Wrap with tulle and finish with a knotted ribbon and a marbled nail polish gift tag (page 152).

Lip Care Kit

Alternate a stack of three to five Coconut Lip Balms (page 94) and Vanilla Coffee Lip Scrubs (page 92). Stack containers, then wrap with tulle and finish with a knotted ribbon and a marbled nail polish gift tag (page 152).

Sugar Scrub Trio

Pair together the Chocolate Sugar Hand Scrub (page 16), Gingerbread Foot Scrub (page 34) and Vanilla Honey Shower Scrub (page 52) for a sugary sweet gift! Package the product into 120-ml glass canning jars. Finish with coordinating labels and washi tape to line the screw-top lids (page 151).

CONGRATS TO YOU!

You've made all-natural recipes that beautify your mind and body. Which one was your favourite? The calming or the rejuvenating? The scrubbing or the soothing?

It's important to pamper yourself every week – if not every day. Taking even just 5 minutes to relax with one of your favourite recipes can relieve stress, calm your nerves and help you find focus.

Once you've spoiled yourself, don't forget to share the love by giving away these beauty products as gifts. Or throw a party and pamper your guests with spa-like treatments.

It's all about feeling beautiful in the skin you're in. When you feel beautiful, you look beautiful!

ABOUT THE AUTHOR

Aubre Andrus is an award-winning children's book author. She cherishes her time spent as the Lifestyle Editor of *American Girl* magazine where she developed crafts, recipes and party ideas for girls. When she's not writing, Aubre loves travelling around the world, and some of her favourite places include India, Cambodia and Japan. She currently lives in Los Angeles, USA, with her husband. You can find her website at www.aubreandrus.com.

Published by Curious Fox, an imprint of Capstone Global Library Limited,
264 Banbury Road, Oxford, OX2 7DY – Registered company number: 6695582

www.curious-fox.com

ISBN 978 1 78202 607 5

21 20 19 18 17
10 9 8 7 6 5 4 3 2 1

A CIP catalogue for this book is available from the British Library.

Image Credits: Photographs by Capstone Studio:
Karon Dubke, photographer; Sarah Schuette, photo stylist;
Marcy Morin, studio scheduler;
Author photo by Ariel Andrus

Printed and bound in China.